Rectangles

Seeing Rectangles All Around Us

by Sarah L. Schuette

Reading Consultant:

Elena Bodrova, Ph.D., Senior Consultant

Mid-continent Research for Education and Learning

Capstone press

North Mankato, Minnesota

A+ Books are published by Capstone Press,
1710 Roe Crest Drive, North Mankato, Minnesota 56003.
www.capstonepub.com

Copyright 2003 by Capstone Press, a Capstone imprint. All rights reserved.
No part of this publication may be reproduced in whole or in part, or stored in a retrieval system, or transmitted in any form or by any means, electronic, mechanical, photocopying, recording, or otherwise, without written permission of the publisher. For information regarding permission, write to Capstone Press, 1710 Roe Crest Drive, North Mankato, Minnesota 56003.

Library of Congress Cataloging-in-Publication Data
Schuette, Sarah L., 1976–
Rectangles: Seeing rectangles all around us / by Sarah L. Schuette.
p.cm—(Shapes)
Summary: Simple text, photographs, and illustrations show rectangles in everyday objects.
Includes bibliographical references and index.
ISBN-13: 978-0-7368-1462-1 (hardcover) ISBN-10: 0-7368-1462-0 (hardcover)
ISBN-13: 978-0-7368-5060-5 (softcover pbk.) ISBN-10: 0-7368-5060-0 (softcover pbk.)
I. Rectangle—Juvenile literature. [1.Rectangle.] I. Title.
QA482 .S38 2003
516'.15—dc21 2002000893

Created by the A+ Team
Sarah L. Schuette, editor; Heather Kindseth, art director and designer; Jason Knudson, designer and illustrator; Angi Gahler, illustrator; Gary Sundermeyer, photographer; Nancy White, photo stylist

Note to Parents, Teachers, and Librarians
The Shapes series uses color photographs and a nonfiction format to introduce children to the shapes around them. It is designed to be read aloud to a pre-reader or to be read independently by an early reader. The images help early readers and listeners understand the text and concepts discussed. The book encourages further the following sections: Table of Contents, Words to Know, Read More, Internet Sites, and Index. Early readers may need assistance using these features.

Printed in the United States 5559

Table of Contents

Rectangles	4
Seeing Rectangles	10
Rectangle Money	14
More Rectangles	18
Build a Rectangle Town	28
Words to Know	30
Read More	31
Internet Sites	31
Index	32

Rectangles

Rectangles have four sides,
two short and two long.

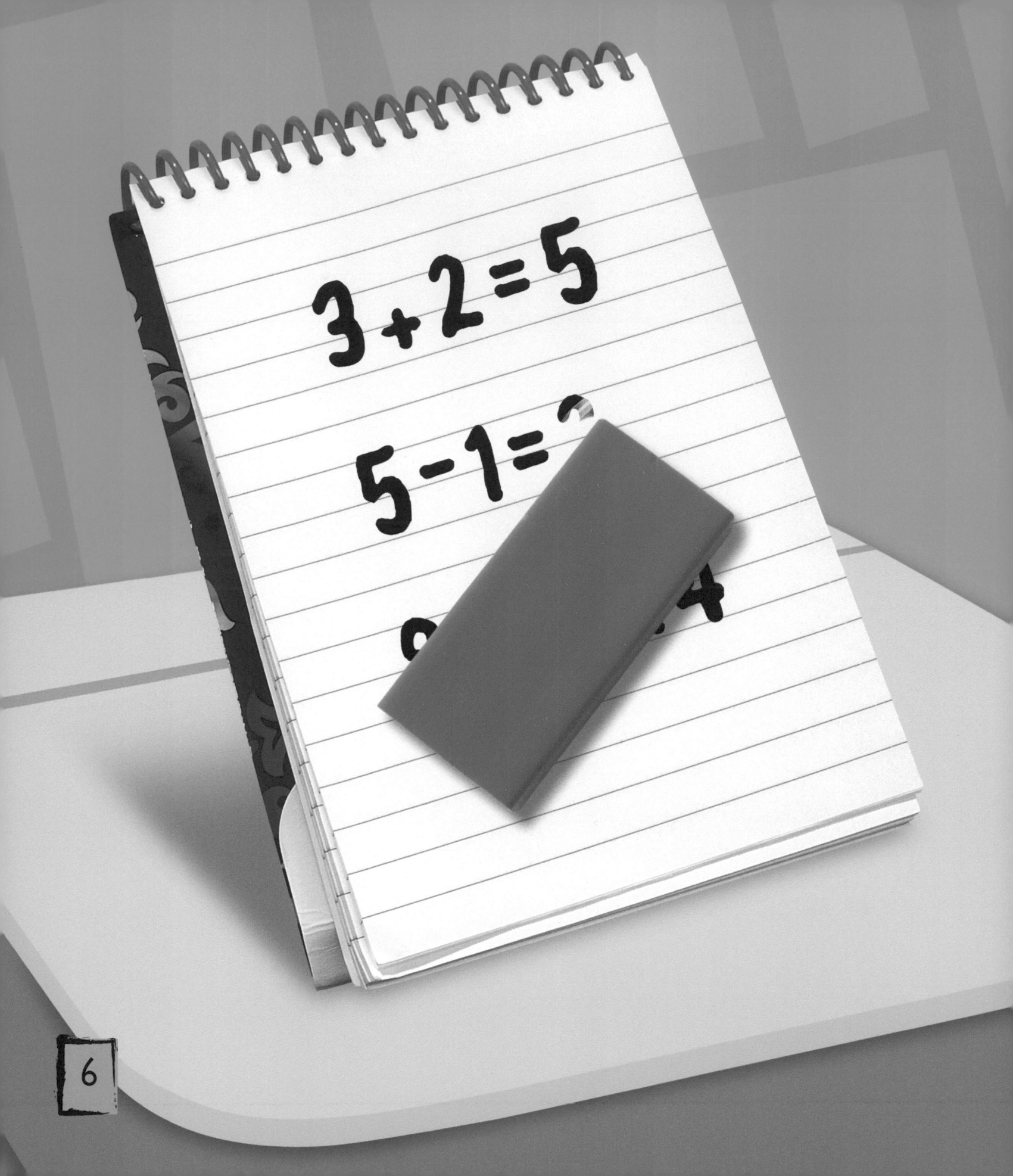
3+2=5
5-1=

Everyone makes mistakes. Luckily, you can easily fix mistakes on your homework with an eraser.

They rub out the answers you write that are wrong.

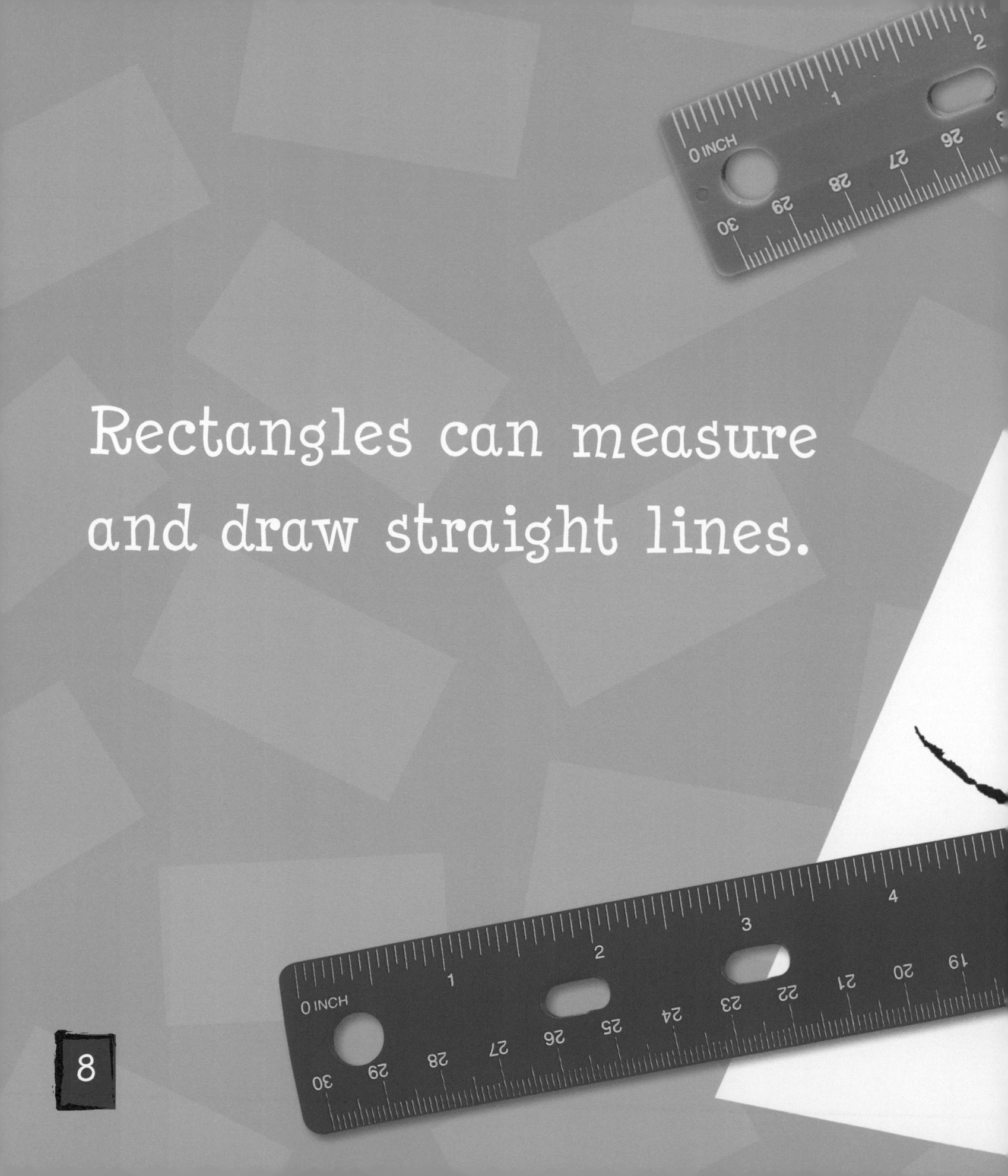

Rectangles can measure and draw straight lines.

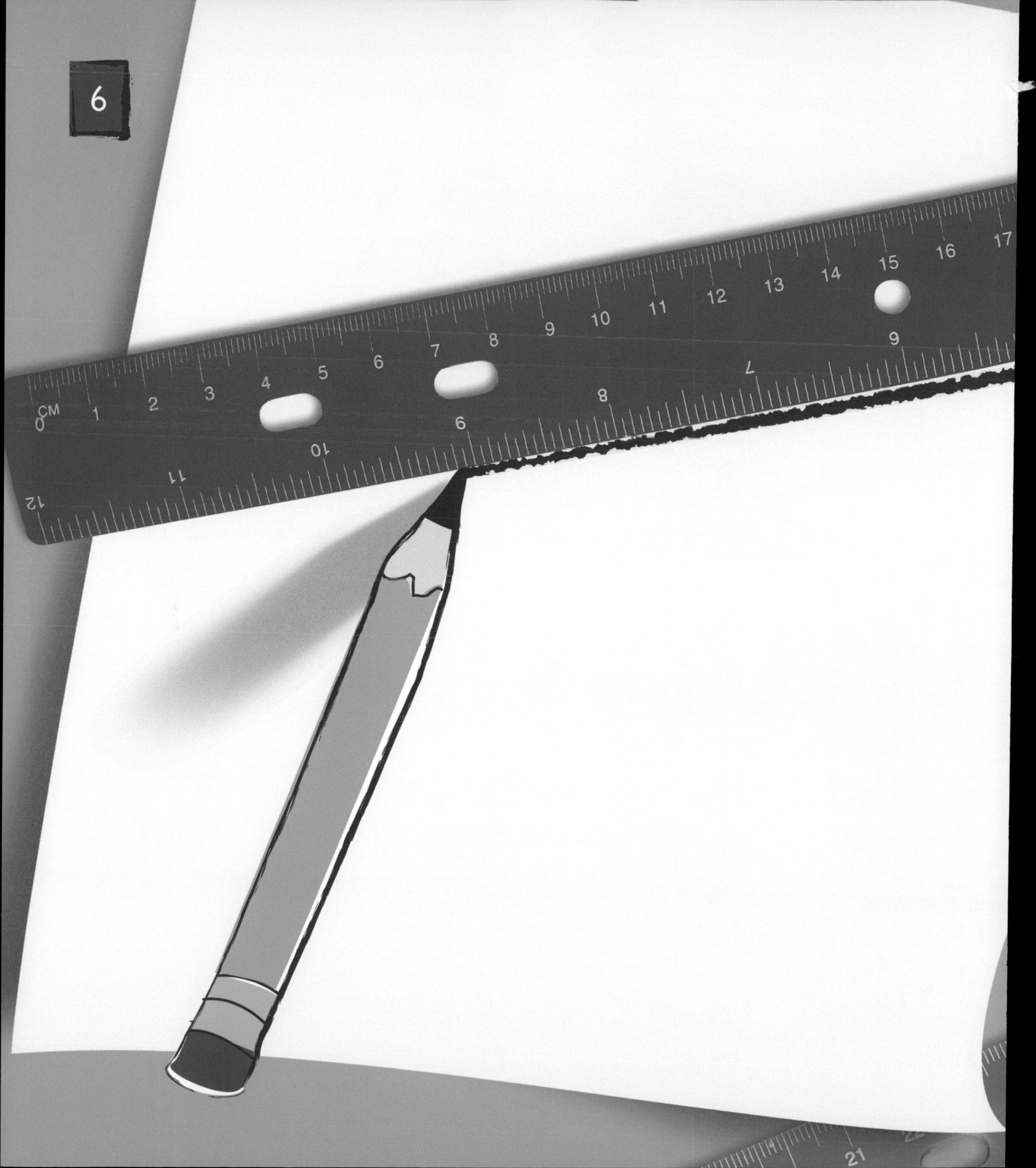
CM
0 1 2 3 4 5 6 7 8 9 10 11 12 13 14 15 16 17

SPEED
LIMIT
45

Speed limit signs tell drivers about safe speeds. Traffic signs come in many different shapes and colors.

Rectangles are white speed limit signs.

Fifty-two rectangles make up a deck.

10
J
3
10
A
J
6
A
5
Q
3
8
2

Happy
Birthday

On your birthday, you might get a check.

Banks will give you money when you exchange a check for cash. Then you can save your money or buy a fun treat.

You use rectangles when you pay.

E93057182 A
WASHINGTON, D.C.
5
Secretary of the Treasury

Did you know that most pianos have 88 black and white keys? Musical notes tell players which keys to press on the piano. Some piano players can even play without reading music.

Piano keys are rectangles you play.

2
3
4
5
6
7
8
9
10
11
12
13
14
15

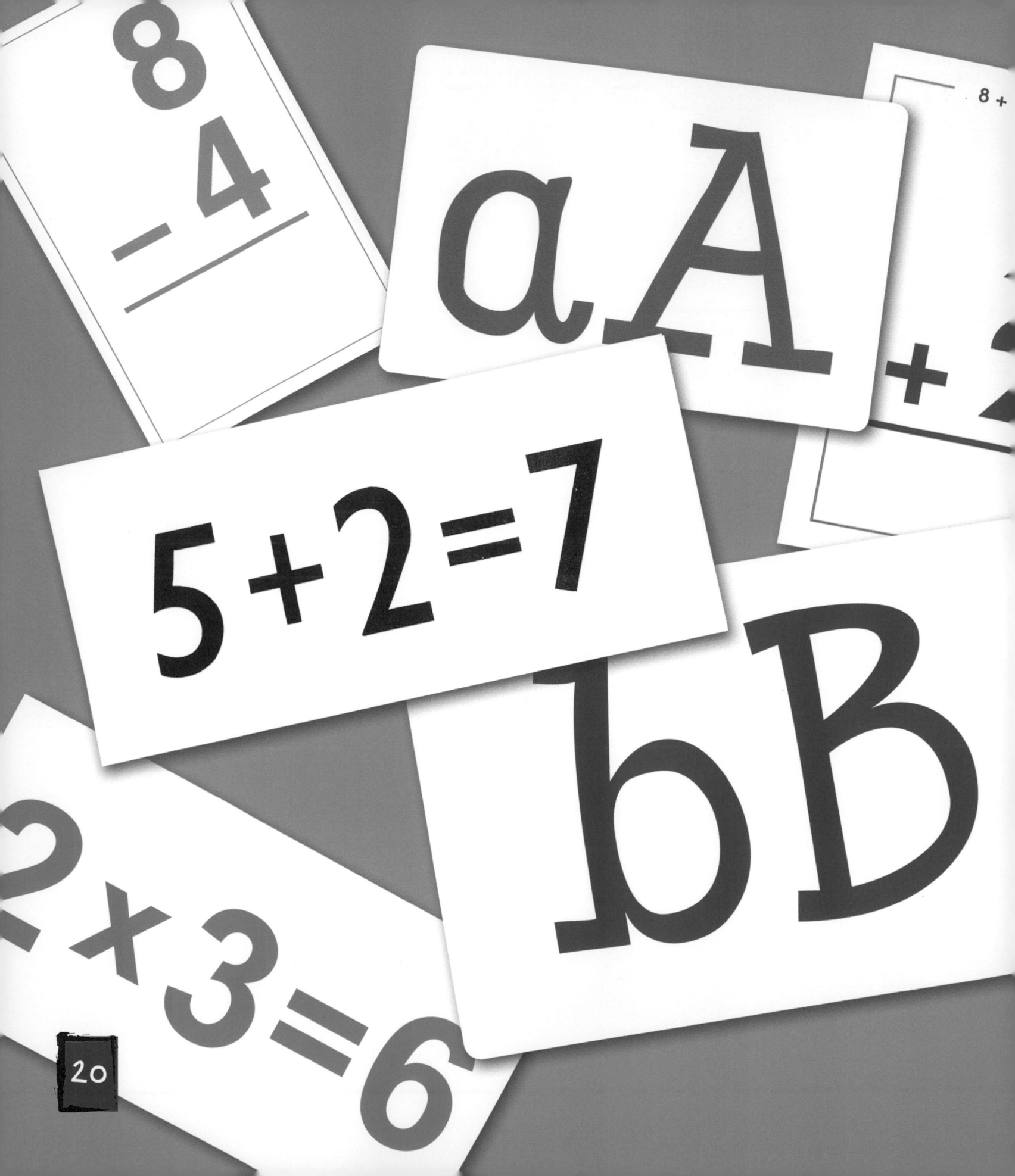
8
- 4
aA
8 +
+ 2
5+2=7
bB
2×3=6

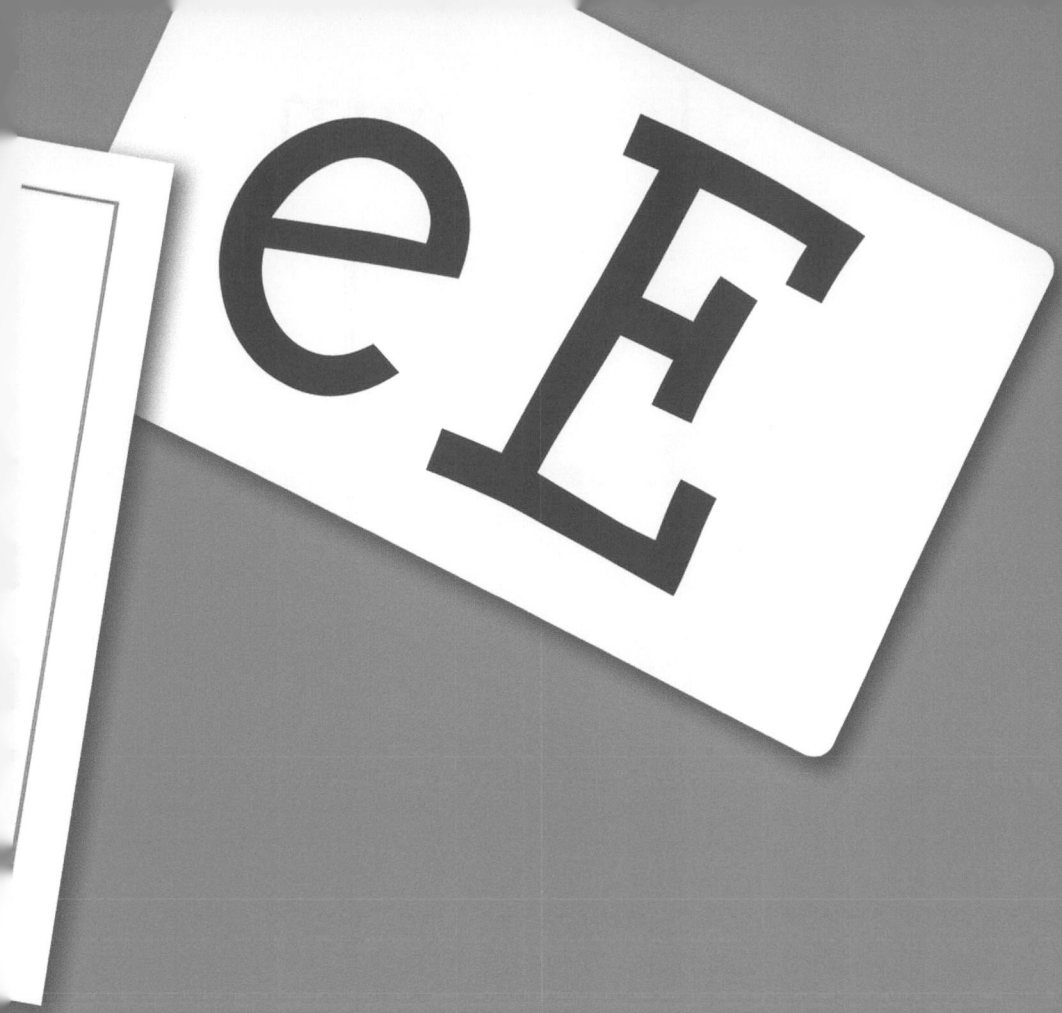

Use flash rectangles at your school.

A rectangle can even float in your pool.

It is fun to chew gum and blow bubbles. If you ever get gum stuck in your hair, use peanut butter to get it out.

Sticks of gum are rectangles you chew.

Find the rectangle that sticks on you.

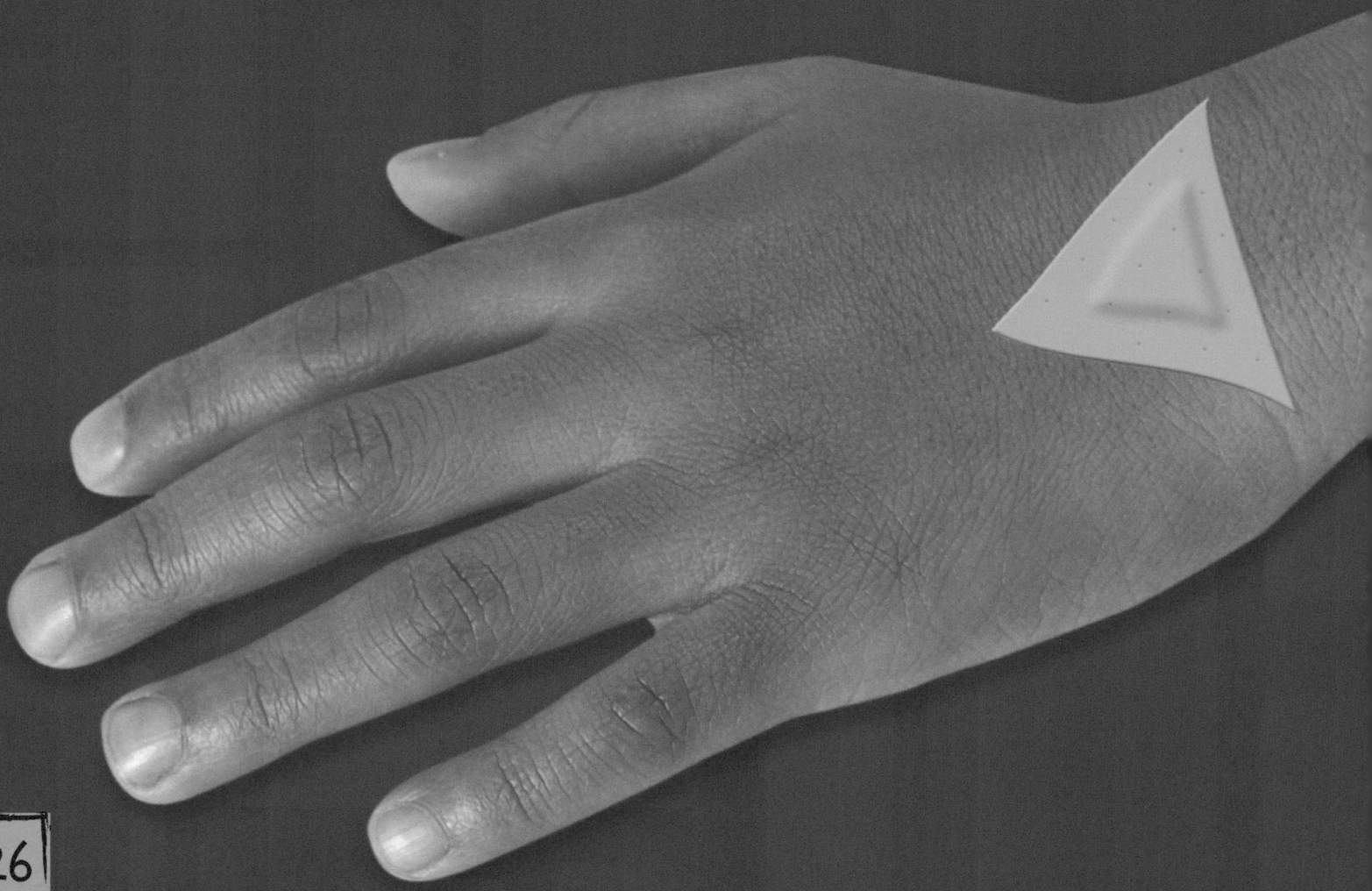

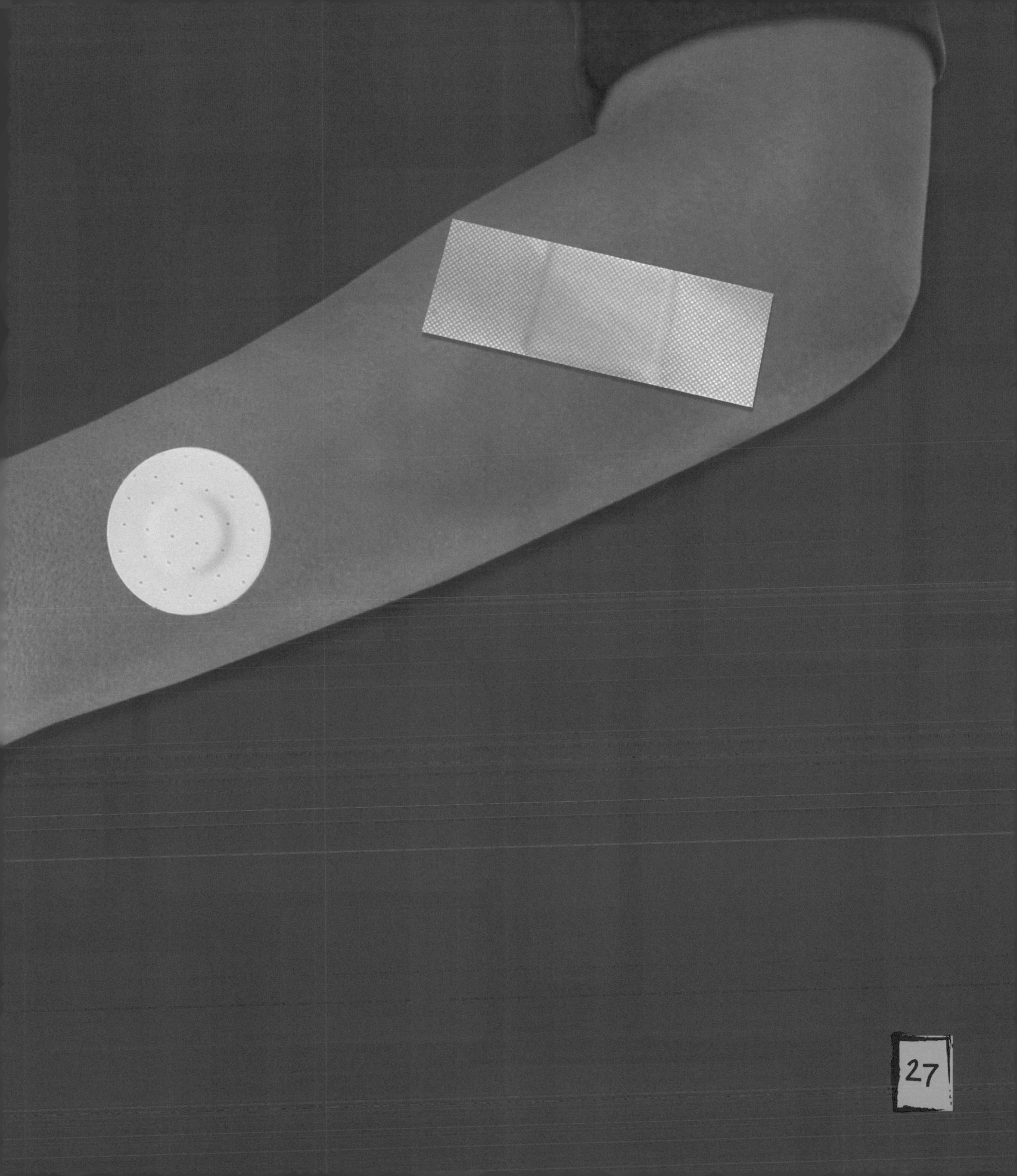

Build a Rectangle Town

1 Break a few of the large crackers into smaller rectangle pieces. Arrange the pieces on the cookie sheet.

2 Spread the frosting on the crackers with the spoon. Add sprinkles.

3 Draw windows and doors with the gel icing. Try making other rectangles that you see in your town.

Words to Know

deck—a full set of playing cards; there are 52 cards in a deck; each card is a rectangle.

exchange—to give one thing and to get something back in return; people can exchange checks for cash at banks.

measure—to find out the size of something; rulers are rectangles that people use to measure or draw straight lines.

note—a written symbol that stands for a musical sound

piano—a large keyboard instrument; pressing down on the black and white keys on a piano makes different sounds.

speed—the rate that something moves; speeds can be slow or fast; speed limit signs are rectangles.

Read More

Burke, Jennifer S. *Rectangles.* City Shapes. New York: Children's Press, 2000.

Patilla, Peter. *Starting Off with Shapes.* Hauppauge, New York: Barron's, 2001.

Ross, Kathy. *Kathy Ross Crafts Triangles, Rectangles, Circles, and Squares.* Learning Is Fun! Brookfield, Conn.: Millbrook Press, 2002.

Yates, Irene. *All about Shapes.* New York: Benchmark Books, 1998.

Internet Sites

Track down many sites about rectangles.

IT IS EASY! IT IS FUN!

1) Go to *http://www.facthound.com*
2) Type in: 0736814620
3) Click on "FETCH IT" and FACT HOUND will find several links hand-picked by our editors.

Relax and let our pal FACT HOUND do the research for you!

Index

banks, 15
check, 15
eraser, 7
gum, 25
hair, 25
homework, 7
keys, 18
money, 15
music, 18
peanut butter, 25
piano, 18
pool, 23
school, 21
speed limit signs, 11

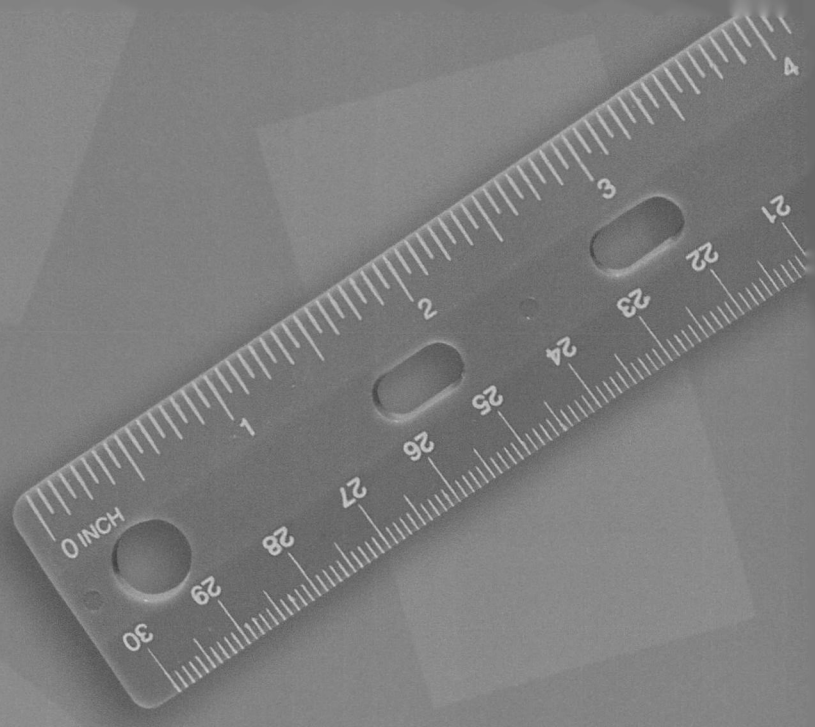